THE POMO

NIA KENNEDY

PowerKiDS press™

NEW YORK

Published in 2018 by The Rosen Publishing Group, Inc.
29 East 21st Street, New York, NY 10010

Editor: Melissa Raé Shofner
Book Design: Michael Flynn
Interior Layout: Rachel Rising

Photo Credits: Cover Marilyn Angel Wynn/Corbis Documentary/Getty Images; pp. 5, 9, 13, 27, 29 Courtesy of the Library of Congress; p. 7 Buyenlarge/Archive Photos/Getty Images; p. 10 https://commons.wikimedia.org/wiki/File:Girl%27s_Coiled_Dowry_or_Puberty_Basket_(kol-chu_or_ti-ri-bu-ku),_late_19th_century,07.467.8308.jpg; p. 11 Photo Lot 89-8, National Anthropological Archives, Smithsonian Institution; p. 15 Art Collection 3/Alamy Stock Photo; p. 16 Marilyn Angel Wynn/Nativestock/Getty Images; p. 17 DEA PICTURE LIBRARY/De Agostini/Getty Images; p. 18 https://commons.wikimedia.org/wiki/File:Doctor%27s_Headdress_(guk-tsu-shua),_Pomo_(Native_American),_1906-1907C.E.,_08.491.8952.jpg; pp. 19, 25 Courtesy of the USC Digital Library; p. 21 alexbroker01/Shutterstock.com; p. 23 Mariusz S. Jurgielewicz/Shutterstock.com.

Cataloging-in-Publication Data

Names: Kennedy, Nia.
Title: The Pomo / Nia Kennedy.
Description: New York : PowerKids Press, 2018. | Series: Spotlight on the American Indians of California | Includes index.
Identifiers: ISBN 9781508162902 (pbk.) | ISBN 9781538324882 (library bound) | ISBN 9781508162957 (6 pack)
Subjects: LCSH: Pomo Indians--Juvenile literature.
Classification: LCC E99.P65 K46 2018 | DDC 979.4004'97574--dc23

Manufactured in China

CPSIA Compliance Information: Batch #BW18PK For further information contact Rosen Publishing, New York, New York at 1-800-237-9932.

CONTENTS

CHAPTER ONE

THE EARLY POMO

The early Pomo Indians lived in Northern California in parts of modern Mendocino, Sonoma, and Lake Counties. They divided themselves into seven groups. Each had its own language, **customs**, and traditions. Because the languages of these groups had many similar features, scholars have collectively called these people the Pomo. Prior to contact with Europeans, the seven groups didn't describe themselves as a single group. However, since 1851, most of them call themselves the Pomo.

Scholars estimate that, in 1800, there were likely more than 8,000 Pomo in Northern California. Since that time, the Pomo have faced many challenges, including repeated invasions of their land. As more newcomers arrived, the Pomo, along with other American Indians, were killed or forced to leave their lands. By 1900, the Pomo had lost control of nearly all their land. Today, they continue to fight for their civil rights and fair treatment.

Throughout their history, the Pomo people have been hunters, fishermen, warriors, craftspeople, and traders. Their story is one of hard work and courage.

POMO MAN
IN TRADITIONAL
DANCE COSTUME, 1924

5

CHAPTER TWO

VILLAGE LIFE

Each of the regions in which the seven Pomo groups lived contained many villages. Small villages had as few as 12 homes, while larger villages could have more than 100. The Pomo built their homes in different styles using different materials depending on where they lived.

Every Pomo village had a sweathouse. These round structures were built inside a pit and covered with a layer of earth. Inside, a fire filled the space with smoke and heat. Men took daily sweat baths for cleansing, healing, and enjoyment. In some communities, the men slept and spent most of their free time in the sweathouse.

There was at least one assembly house in each village. Assembly houses were used for ceremonies and meetings. These buildings had a special section of wall that could be pushed away for a quick escape in case of an emergency, such as a fire.

The Pomo often spent part of the year away from their villages in places where food was available. They lived in temporary campsites in shelters made of poles and thatch.

CHAPTER THREE

PREPARING MEALS

The Pomo used a number of methods to prepare their meals. They often used pit ovens. To make one of these ovens, they dug a hole in the ground and built a fire inside. After a while, the fuel was removed to put out the fire, leaving the rocks and soil hot enough to cook the food. The food, which was usually wrapped in leaves, was put inside the hole and covered with hot rocks. After a few hours, the meal was ready to eat.

The early Pomo were also experts at cooking stews inside tightly woven baskets using hot rocks. Acorns and dried plants were stored in baskets or similar containers. The Pomo preserved all their leftover food for later use or trade. They salted or smoked fish and meat to prevent these foods from spoiling.

Most Pomo often prepared their meals outside. They usually cooked over an open flame, but some foods were grilled, smoked, or steamed.

CHAPTER FOUR

BEAUTIFUL BASKETS

The Pomo Indians were experts at making beautiful crafts and useful tools. The women collected many kinds of grasses and other plants to weave into baskets decorated with **geometric** patterns. Beads and feathers were sometimes added for extra decoration. Many types and sizes of baskets were produced, including plates, bowls, and jars.

Many experts believe the Pomo created, and continue to make, the finest baskets on Earth.

Obsidian, a glass-like volcanic rock, was skillfully chipped into arrowheads, drills, knives, and various other cutting tools. The surfaces of special rocks called magnesite were smoothed to make beautiful beads. Wood, bark, and reeds were also used to make items such as bows, cloth, and smoking pipes.

The Pomo made many useful things from the animals they hunted. They used animal skins to make blankets and clothing. Bones were crafted into jewelry, fishhooks, and other items. They also made items from seashells and bird feathers.

CHAPTER FIVE

POMO SOCIETY

Extended families were the smallest social groups in Pomo communities. When a couple married, they could move near either the husband or wife's family. It was common for extended families to unite into a single larger group that was headed by the oldest family members. Most villages included several larger family units. Household chores were usually assigned based on a person's age and if they were male or female.

Outside the home, most men and many women had jobs. There were bead makers, hunters, basket makers, bow-and-arrow makers, and more. Each group formed its own trade organization. A person had to study many years before they could join or practice without **supervision**.

The wealthiest and most powerful men were the political leaders, often called chiefs.

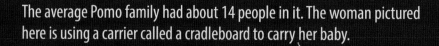

The average Pomo family had about 14 people in it. The woman pictured here is using a carrier called a cradleboard to carry her baby.

CHAPTER SIX

DIFFERENT GOVERNMENTS

The village community was the basic unit of government for the Pomo people. Each of the seven original groups had their own lands and a central settlement. The largest Pomo group may have had a number of smaller, independent villages and as many as 2,000 total members.

The system of government of each early Pomo group was different. In some communities, there was a single major leader, or chief. In other Pomo villages, a chief had several aides. Some leaders inherited their positions, while others were elected by the community's adults. In some communities, the oldest people from each extended family came together with others to form a village council, or assembly.

Pomo villages sometimes formed temporary **alliances** with each other. This meant that a few leaders had control of multiple villages for short periods of time. These alliances often quickly broke down.

Religious and medical leaders were also important in Pomo society. The most powerful of these men and women were known as bear doctors.

CHAPTER SEVEN

POMO WARRIORS

Warfare was important to the early Pomo people. Some wars began when religious leaders of one community performed **rituals** designed to hurt the people of another village. Once one side had been defeated or hurt, the other side often wanted revenge.

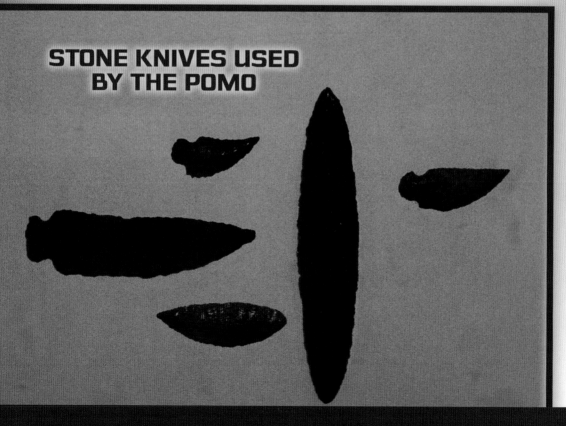

STONE KNIVES USED BY THE POMO

The Pomo people started wars over many things, such as control of land and natural resources.

To prepare for battle, Pomo warriors held religious ceremonies in which they prayed and worshiped with special dances and songs. The religious leaders tried to use **supernatural** powers to **predict** what would happen during the fighting. Sometimes a war was settled by a ritual battle in which armies came together at a chosen place to trade insults and arrows.

These ritual battles ended when someone was killed. In exchange for peace, the losers had to give something up. The winning warriors sometimes held special ceremonies to celebrate their victory.

CHAPTER EIGHT

RITUALS AND HEALING

Religion was an important part of life for the Pomo people. From the time they were born, young people were taught songs, dances, and religious stories. Religion helped the Pomo make sense of the world and learn how to be good people. Most of their holidays and rituals were connected to their religious beliefs.

POMO DOCTOR'S HEADDRESS

The early Pomo people believed certain places in nature had special powers. This rock was thought to help women have babies.

The Pomo held special ceremonies to bring them power, health, and good fortune. There were also many ceremonies for boys and girls that marked special occasions as they grew up. Beautiful religious services marked the passing of the seasons.

Pomo religious leaders spent much of their time working as doctors. They often treated sick people by using special plants and performing rituals, special songs, and dances. People paid the doctors in goods or bead money. Doctors were sometimes feared because it was believed they could hurt people with poisons. Many of the Pomo people still practice their religion today.

CHAPTER NINE

RUSSIAN NEWCOMERS

Between 1542 and 1812, the ships of many different European countries sailed by the Pomo lands. Many were Spanish merchant vessels. After 1750, Spain and Russia began their expansion efforts in North America.

The Russians were the first newcomers to meet the Pomo people. In 1812, they established Fort Ross along the coast in present-day Sonoma County. The Russians didn't want to control California the way the Spanish did. They were more interested in creating farms and ranches and making money by collecting and selling seal and sea otter skins.

At first, the Russians and the Pomo got along well. The Pomo considered the Russians to be good trading partners and military **allies**. The Russians helped keep the Spaniards and other Pomo enemies away. However, in 1830, troops at Fort Ross forced the Pomo to work without pay. This ruined the good relationship between the Russians and the Pomo people.

The Russian American Fur Company owned Fort Ross. In 1841, the company decided that the cost of keeping the colony was greater than the profits it was making. The Russians closed the fort and sold the buildings to the Mexican government.

CHAPTER TEN

THE SPANISH MISSIONS

King Carlos III of Spain sent people to take control of California in 1769. It wasn't until about 1817, however, that Spanish explorers arrived in Pomo territory. Spanish officials wanted to block the Russians and expand their control of California. The Spanish built **missions** to convince Spain's American Indian allies to adopt the Christian religion and European lifestyle. However, the mission program in Mexico territory, which California was a part of at the time, ended when the country gained independence from Spain in 1821.

By 1823, Europeans and members of various other American Indian groups frequently passed through Pomo territory, bringing new ideas and trade goods as well as deadly diseases. In 1822, the Mexican government began to give private ranches in Pomo territory to retired soldiers. The new ranches would help Mexico keep its hold on California. The remaining missions were quickly turned into new kinds of settlements.

Some Southern Pomo people moved to Mission San Rafael, which was built in 1817. Over the next 18 years, at least 600 members of the Northern Pomo group also moved to missions. Scholars aren't sure what mission life was like for the Pomo people.

CHAPTER ELEVEN

TROUBLE WITH MEXICO

After 1835, California's system of government broke down, and wealthy landowners fought over who would rule. Ranchers thought the American Indians should be slaves and treated them very poorly.

Many people living at the missions escaped to the east and organized **raiding** parties with other American Indian groups. Between 1835 and 1847, these raiders stole thousands of horses and cattle from Mexican towns and ranches. Many of the settlements had to be abandoned.

Changes in government policies meant that Mission San Francisco Solano de Sonoma was turned into a military base ruled by Mariano Guadalupe Vallejo. To expand Mexican control, Vallejo gave ranches to his followers and family members.

Between 1835 and 1847, many Pomo people died while fighting or because of harsh treatment or diseases. Thousands of others became slaves. For the Pomo communities that managed to survive, the hard times were just beginning.

Mariano Guadalupe Vallejo was a military commander of the Republic of Mexico. He hoped to expand Mexico's control over the California area, block the Russians, and conquer the Pomo people.

CHAPTER TWELVE

THE UNSTOPPABLE UNITED STATES

The U.S.-Mexican War (1846–1848) ended with a treaty that forced Mexico to transfer control of California to the United States. Things didn't improve for the American Indians under the new government, which denied nearly all American Indian people, including the Pomo, their basic human rights. Some American officials believed that the American Indians should be exterminated, or killed off.

From 1850 through 1900, nearly all the Pomo lands were stolen by gold rush settlers who found valuable resources there. Many of the defeated Pomo people were forced to move to the Mendocino Indian **Reservation** or the Round Valley Reservation because they had nowhere else to go.

By the end of the 19th century, many Pomo people had saved enough money to purchase land and rebuild their old communities. Legal problems soon threatened the new settlements, but the Pomo people continued to fight for their rights.

Some Pomo people worked for very little pay and were allowed to live outside the government reserves in new communities called rancherías. When they weren't working, many Pomo people tried to preserve their ancient ways of life.

CHAPTER THIRTEEN

CHANGES IN THE 20TH CENTURY

By the beginning of the 20th century, the outsiders' hatred toward the Pomo people had started to **decline**. Life began improving for the Pomo people. After 1910, U.S. government officials began a new policy of working to create reservations for the homeless American Indians of California. Over the next 10 years, 52 new communities were created, including several Pomo rancherías.

In 1924, American Indians were granted the full benefits of United States citizenship, including the right to vote. After World War II ended, however, American Indians faced new challenges. Some government officials wanted to get rid of the reservation system.

In 1966, the government closed a number of reservations and divided the lands among the people who had lived there. Yet again, the Pomo people found it necessary to organize themselves to preserve and protect their rights.

When the reservations closed years later, the lack of government support may have made it harder for many Pomo people, like the man shown here, to preserve their culture.

CHAPTER FOURTEEN

THE POMO PEOPLE TODAY

In 1990, nearly 5,000 people identified themselves as members of the Pomo people. Ancient customs remain important to the Pomo, both on and off reservations. Family life continues to be the focus of many traditions. Large numbers of young Pomo people are learning their ancient languages and taking part in traditional activities, such as dancing, singing, storytelling, basket making, and cooking. The artwork of the Pomo is respected throughout the world. Pomo doctors continue to treat patients with ancient methods.

The Pomo have dealt with many hardships over the last several centuries, and they continue to face challenges today. Even with their great efforts and many victories, the Pomo people are often still denied the rights that are extended to other American Indians and U.S. citizens. Today, the Pomo continue to fight for the rights and respect they deserve.

GLOSSARY

alliance (uh-LY-unts) A close association formed between people or groups of people to reach a common objective.

ally (AA-ly) One of two or more people or groups who work together.

custom (KUS-tuhm) An action or way of behaving that is traditional among the people in a certain group or place.

decline (dih-KLYN) To become less in amount.

geometric (jee-uh-MEH-trik) Having to do with straight lines, circles, and other simple shapes.

mission (MIH-shun) A community established by a church for the purpose of spreading its faith.

predict (prih-DIKT) To guess what will happen in the future based on facts or knowledge.

raid (RAYD) To make a surprise attack on someone.

reservation (reh-zuhr-VAY-shun) Land set aside by the government for specific American Indian nations to live on.

ritual (RIH-choo-uhl) A religious ceremony, especially one consisting of a series of actions performed in a certain order.

supernatural (soo-pur-NAH-chur-uhl) Unable to be explained by science or the laws of nature.

supervision (soo-per-VIH-zhun) The act of watching and directing what someone does or how something is done.

INDEX

PRIMARY SOURCE LIST

Page 7
Construction of a tule shelter, Lake Pomo. Photograph. Edward S. Curtis. 1924. Now held at the Library of Congress Prints and Photographs Division, Washington, D.C.

Page 13
Pomo man and woman with baby and dog. Photograph. ca. 1905. Now held at the Library of Congress Prints and Photographs Division, Washington, D.C.

Page 25
Mariano Guadalupe Vallejo. Photograph. I. W. Taber. ca. 1880–1885. Now held by the Bancroft Library, University of California, Berkeley, CA.

WEBSITES

Due to the changing nature of Internet links, PowerKids Press has developed an online list of websites related to the subject of this book. This site is updated regularly. Please use this link to access the list: www.powerkidslinks.com/saic/pomo